What's the Big Idea?

Four Centuries of Innovation in Boston

STEPHEN KRENSKY

What's the Big Idea?

Four Centuries of Innovation in Boston

STEPHEN KRENSKY

**Published in partnership with
the Boston History & Innovation Collaborative**

ini Charlesbridge

For my father, Boston Latin, Class of 1944—S. K.

Published by Charlesbridge
85 Main Street
Watertown, MA 02472
(617) 926-0329
www.charlesbridge.com

Library of Congress Cataloging-in-Publication Data
Krensky, Stephen.
   What's the big idea? : four centuries of innovation in Boston / Stephen
Krensky.
      p. cm.
   ISBN 978-1-58089-310-7 (reinforced for library use)
   ISBN 978-1-58089-311-4 (softcover)
1. Boston (Mass.)—Economic conditions. 2. Cities and towns—Effect of
technological innovations on—Massachusetts—Boston—History. 3. Urban
policy—Massachusetts—Boston—History. I. Title.
HC108.B65K74 2007
330.9774'61—dc22   2006021255

Printed in Singapore
(hc) 10 9 8 7 6 5 4 3 2 1
(sc) 10 9 8 7 6 5 4 3 2 1

Display type and text type set in Bailey Sans and New Caledonia
Printed and bound by Imago
Production supervision by Brian G. Walker
Designed by Susan Mallory Sherman and Martha MacLeod Sikkema

Contents

Boston city seal

Introduction

Whatʼs new in Boston? Quite a lot, actually. And itʼs been that way ever since the city was founded in 1630. Innovations are fresh ideas that push or pull people in new directions. Innovations have always marked Bostonʼs progress. People who made innovations have had many reasons. Some innovators were driven by scientific curiosity. Others wanted to improve society. Some hoped to make money. Whatever their motives, they all took risks to further their goals.

Of course, not every change happens in the same way. Sometimes an innovation is simply a new invention—like the first telephone. An innovation can be a major improvement, too, like the one that made a lightbulb last for eight hours instead of eight minutes. Itʼs also an innovation to use an existing idea in a new way. For example, a gas called nitrous oxide was putting people to sleep long before anyone thought to use it to help out in medical surgeries.

View from Boston Harbor

Boston is special. It has the ocean on one side and unlimited possibilities on the other. It's a place where things happen. So keep your eyes open—and take a closer look.

1. A Fresh Start

Painting of Tremount, or "three hills" of Boston, as it was in 1630

In 1630 almost 1,000 Puritans arrived in Boston Harbor. They came together on a small fleet of boats led by the *Arbella*.

Boston in the 1600s was a very busy place. Fishing boats came and went with the tides. Merchants sold goods in the market. New buildings were sprouting up everywhere, from the wharves on Town Dock to the houses at the base of Beacon Hill.

The Puritans who built Boston had been unhappy in England. They thought their king, Charles I, was leading their religion in the wrong direction. Kings, of course, don't like to be criticized. So the Puritans came to America, where Charles would leave them alone.

Puritans didn't smile much. And they were pretty strict. They did not allow music and dancing. Children were not supposed to speak at meals.

Above all, the Puritans believed in hard work. And for that they had come to the right place. Life in New England was challenging. The winters were harsh, and the summers were hot. As for the Native Americans, they were here first and were weary of these pushy newcomers. Not all the Native Americans were welcoming.

None of this bothered the Puritan leader John Winthrop. For him, the settlement in Boston was a dream come true. Back in England Winthrop had a comfortable life as a country squire and lawyer, but that wasn't enough to satisfy him. He was afraid that the king and the church were not setting the right example for children. Winthrop wanted to create a society where ordinary men, not just lords and princes, had a voice in governing their own lives.

Winthrop formed the Massachusetts Bay Colony with other people who shared his ideas. Together they made plans to start a new settlement in America. Winthrop wisely asked for and received a charter from the king granting the Massachusetts Bay Colony the right to govern itself. He had already seen that there were always problems when colonies were ruled from far away.

As governor, John Winthrop (1588–1649) wanted the Massachusetts Bay Colony to learn from the bad example of England. He also thought his colony should do a better job than Virginia was doing in letting people govern themselves. Then others would want to come to Boston to be part of his colony.

The ship Mary and John, *one of the vessels that brought settlers to Boston*

Anne Dudley Bradstreet (1612–1672) was a self-taught poet who was published only once in her lifetime. Her collection of poems, *The Tenth Muse Lately Sprung Up in America, By a Gentlewoman of Those Parts,* came out in 1650. The title wasn't Bradstreet's fault. Her brother-in-law had copied her poems secretly and published them in England without her permission. Although she was a devout Puritan, Bradstreet's poems tell of the hard life of a Puritan wife in colonial New England.

After all of Winthrop's preparations, the Puritans had arrived off the Massachusetts coast in June 1630. They had stopped first in Salem before deciding to move a little south to Charlestown. By September of that year the Shawmut Peninsula, with its supply of fresh water, had drawn them to the area they called Boston.

Fresh water, however, did not solve all their problems. In that first winter alone, more than two hundred settlers died from diseases and harsh conditions, leaving only about eight hundred. Another one hundred returned to England the next spring. Those who stayed made it through that winter and were soon joined by others. By the end of the 1630s, more than sixteen thousand colonists were living in Massachusetts.

Reproduction of an engraving by Paul Revere, drawn by Joshua Chadwick, titled "A Westerly view of the colleges in Cambridge, New England"

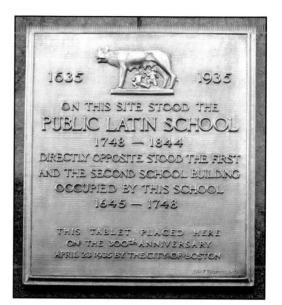

1635   1935

ON THIS SITE STOOD THE
PUBLIC LATIN SCHOOL
1748 — 1844
DIRECTLY OPPOSITE STOOD THE FIRST
AND THE SECOND SCHOOL BUILDING
OCCUPIED BY THIS SCHOOL
1645 — 1748

THIS TABLET PLACED HERE
ON THE 300ᵗʰ ANNIVERSARY
APRIL 23 1935 BY THE CITY OF BOSTON

John Winthrop had high hopes for the new community. He did not want it to be simply a place of business. Winthrop wanted Boston to be something greater, an example of a better society. "We must consider that we shall be a City upon a Hill. The eyes of all people are upon us," he wrote. And he spent the rest of his life trying to make his vision for Boston a reality.

The Puritans believed that education was important to society. They built America's first school, Boston Latin School, in 1635. That same year, John Harvard, a Puritan church leader, died. He left the colony his library and enough money to build America's first college, Harvard. For nearly 60 years, Harvard was the only college in the British North American colonies.

2. Scratching the Surface

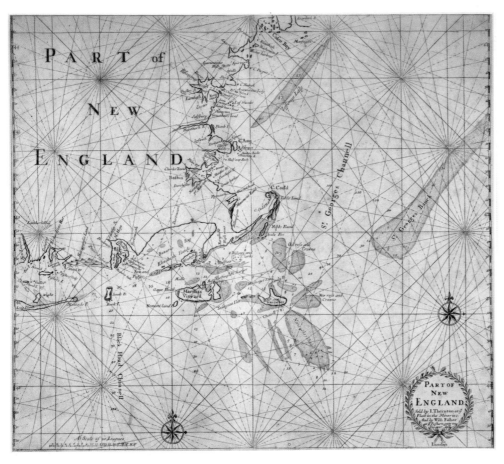

Chart of part of New England from
The English Pilot (1698)

Change filled the Boston air in the early 1700s. The Puritans were still in charge, but their control had weakened. The English government now took a greater interest in what was happening in its colonies. Colonies were supposed to make money for the mother country. If profits were being made in New England, England's rulers wanted to make sure they got their share.

Luckily there was plenty of money to share. Fishing and shipbuilding were becoming big businesses in Boston. The port was booming, and a thriving trade had developed with both England and the West Indies.

Little Brewster Island and lighthouse in Boston Harbor

More trade meant many more ships entering and leaving Boston Harbor. It was not always a safe journey, and many ships were shipwrecked. The first lighthouse in America was the Boston Light. It was built in 1716 to keep ships safe from the rocky Massachusetts coast. It was the latest technology of the time. The first lighthouse keeper drowned in a gale, and a 12-year-old Benjamin Franklin wrote a poem about the tragedy that made Franklin famous in the town.

Painting of Captain Kidd by Howard Pyle

Pirates often attacked ships on their way to and from the Caribbean. The British navy helped solve this problem by capturing pirate ships and arresting pirates. Boston had its share of pirates at this time. Captain Kidd was the most famous one ever to be brought to trial in Boston.

Engraving of Captain Kidd's body hanging from a scaffold

With so many people coming and going, public health was a major concern. It was important to maintain a fresh water supply and dispose of garbage properly. But the scariest health issue was the threat of a fast-moving disease. A disease that spreads quickly and afflicts a large number of people is called an epidemic.

In May 1721 Boston was hit by a smallpox epidemic. Almost six thousand caught the disease over the next few months. About one in twelve smallpox victims died. At the time, the medical treatment for the disease was mostly prayer and more prayer.

That was not enough for the minister Cotton Mather. He believed the ability to "seize opportunities to do good" was a "talent." He knew he had to find a creative way to stop the spread of the disease. He had nearly lost three of his children in an earlier outbreak of smallpox, and he did not want to take his chances again.

Mather had a slave named Onesimus who had come from the Caribbean islands. Onesimus was

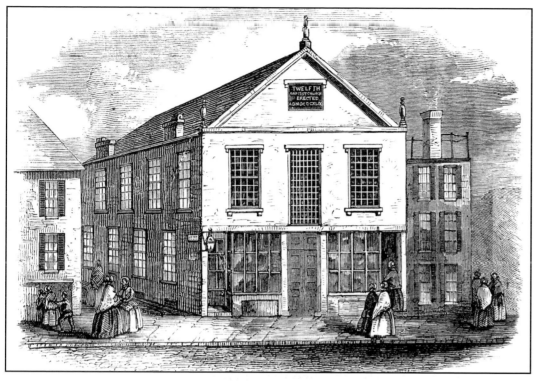

First church in Boston that was built by freed African Americans

Cotton Mather (1663–1728) may have been forward-thinking as a man of science, but he was not happy that people were turning away from the traditional stern Puritan values. This was a big mistake, he thought.

not worried about catching smallpox. He explained to Mather that he had been protected against it in his youth. This was done by actually infecting him with pus from a smallpox victim. Once his body defended itself against this small infection, it would keep defending him against larger ones.

To most people this idea seemed crazy. Why would anyone deliberately spread a disease from one person to another? Wasn't it best to keep sick people away from others? Besides, they observed smugly, this was a slave talking. How could they trust what he said?

Onesimus was an African who had been made a slave in the West Indies before being brought to Boston. In those days, all the colonies, not just the South, allowed slavery. Onesimus was sold as a slave to Cotton Mather in 1706.

AN

Historical ACCOUNT

OF THE

SMALL-POX

INOCULATED

IN

NEW ENGLAND,

Upon all Sorts of Persons, *Whites*, *Blacks*, and of all Ages and Constitutions.

With some Account of the Nature of the Infection in the NATURAL and INOCULATED Way, and their different Effects on HUMAN BODIES.

With some short DIRECTIONS to the UN-EXPERIENCED in this Method of Practice.

Humbly dedicated to her Royal Highness the Princess of WALES,

By *Zabdiel Boylston*, F. R. S.

The Second Edition, Corrected.

L O N D O N:

Printed for S. CHANDLER, at the Cross-Keys in the **Poultry**. M. DCC. XXVI.

Re-Printed at *B O S T O N* in *N. E.* for S. GERRISH in *Cornhil*, and T. HANCOCK at the Bible and **Three Crowns** in *Annstreet*. M. DCC. XXX.

Journal's title page showing the article about Zabdiel Boylston's work to end deaths from smallpox

Cotton Mather wasn't like most people. Neither was his friend, Dr. Zabdiel Boylston. The doctor agreed to test the method of injecting a small amount of the infection, which was called inoculating, on his only son and two slaves. When word got out his neighbors were furious. They claimed Boylston was no better than a murderer. For his own safety the doctor stayed at home to avoid angry citizens on the street.

Fortunately Onesimus was right. The inoculation worked. By midsummer Boylston was using the technique on other people. Two other doctors also began doing it. The death rate from smallpox fell to one person in forty. Clearly inoculations were lifesavers.

Mather, Boylston, and Onesimus were early innovators in Boston. They took a new idea, inoculation, and used it to solve the problem of a smallpox epidemic. The innovation spread, and soon smallpox was no longer

Paul Revere's portrayal of the skirmish, later to become known as the "Boston Massacre," March 5, 1770

Grasshopper weather vane on cupola of Faneuil Hall

a deadly disease. Innovators in Boston had made a difference!

And what did Onesimus get for his help? Well, Mather gave him his freedom, but not for the reason you might think. Cotton Mather thought his slave was not properly obedient. And if Mather wasn't going to put up with smallpox, he certainly wasn't about to put up with that.

Peter Faneuil (1700–1743) became a very successful merchant, although some of his money also came from the slave trade. He proposed building Faneuil Hall, the first public meeting hall and marketplace, as a gift to Boston in 1740. It was completed in 1742, not long before Faneuil's death. It is still used as a lively marketplace on the first floor and meeting hall on the second floor.

3. Change Happens

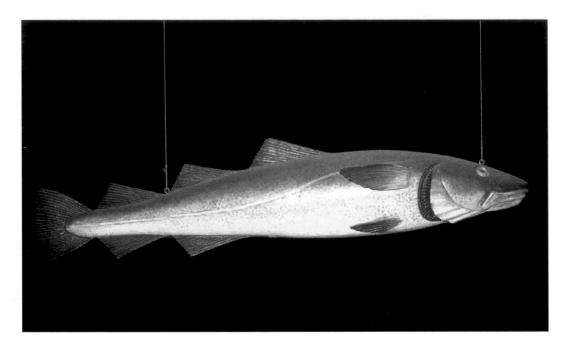

The Sacred Cod, a 5-foot-long fish carved in pine, hangs in the House of Representatives hall of the Massachusetts State House. It is a symbol of the early importance of the fishing industry in Massachusetts.

Some of Boston's success in trade involved sugar and salted fish. And some of it involved slaves. This was not shocking at that time or some big secret. Slavery was legal in Boston and all the British colonies. A few people objected to it, but many did not. A slave was not a person in their eyes. A slave was seen as just another thing to be bought or sold.

The slaves mostly came from Africa, where they were stolen from their homes or villages. Against their will, they were separated from their families, crammed into the hold of a ship, and sent thousands of miles across the ocean. They had only rice and water to eat during the trip. And they were allowed out on deck only twice a day.

Why did all this happen to them? Because selling slaves made a lot of money for a lot of people, who had no interest in giving it up. In fact the idea had never occurred to them.

One young slave who lived through the trip was an eight-year-old girl from Senegal. She arrived in Boston in 1761 on a ship called the *Phillis*. The girl was sold as a slave to Susannah Wheatley, a merchant's wife. It was usual for slaves to be given their owners' names, so she became Phillis Wheatley. (No one asked or cared if she already had a name she would like to keep.)

Since slaves had no rights or privileges, their treatment varied from master to master. Phillis was lucky. Susannah Wheatley was kind to her from the beginning. Susannah saw how quickly Phillis learned to read and write and helped her learn more.

Phillis Wheatley started writing poems when she was twelve. A girl writing poetry at that time was remarkable enough. That a

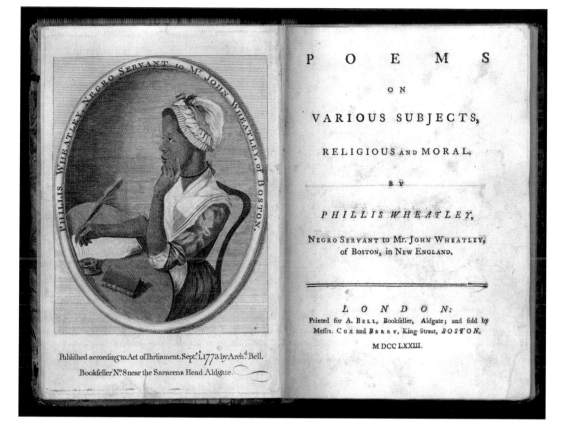

Phillis Wheatley (1753–1784) had her first poem published in 1767. She continued to publish poems until her early death in 1784.

In 1761 there were 16,000 slaves in New England and over 200,000 in all the British North American colonies.

Phillis Wheatley's writing desk

slave girl was doing it was thought to be amazing. And Phillis kept on writing. Susannah showed these poems to her friends. Soon many well-known Bostonians were talking about Phillis.

When Susannah Wheatley decided that Phillis's poems should be published, she faced one big problem. Who would believe a slave girl from Senegal was capable of such work? To prove Phillis was the author, Susannah collected statements from Boston's leading citizens. They said that they knew Phillis and that the poems were truly her own.

Susannah Wheatley was an innovator. Her new idea was that good writing—even by a slave—should be published. Phillis Wheatley's poems were published. People read and liked them. No one knows for sure, but her poetry may have changed some people's ideas about slaves and slavery.

One challenge Phillis Wheatley faced was trying to figure out her place in society. She received a respect no other slave enjoyed, but she still had no rights of her own. In 1773 she visited London. She was treated like a celebrity there, even though under the law she remained the Wheatleys' property. She returned to Boston, and after the publication of her book that same year, the Wheatleys gave Phillis her freedom.

One really important innovation that started in Boston—the creation of a new nation—began as an angry answer to British taxes that the colonists believed were unfair. As the colonists worked together to protest British tax laws, they began to think of themselves as patriots of America, a new country that was separate from Great Britain.

British ships arriving at Long Wharf in 1768

In the 1760s the British created new taxes on stamps, sugar, and even tea. The new taxes were needed because the British expected the colonies to help pay the cost of protecting them from Native American raids. The taxes were very unpopular. In fact, they were an innovation— a new idea—that didn't work.

In 1763 Massachusetts had 184 towns. Boston was the biggest, with a population of around 16,000. Many of the other towns joined Boston in protesting the British taxes.

"The Destruction of Tea at Boston Harbor," 1773

Colonial leaders in Boston staged an innovative act of protest in December 1773. They seized all the tea waiting to be unloaded from ships in Boston Harbor and dumped it into the sea. Their protest worked— the British could not collect taxes on tea at the bottom of the harbor.

Tea leaves in a glass bottle collected on the shore of Dorchester Neck the morning of December 17, 1773

This image of the Declaration of Independence is taken from the engraving made by printer William J. Stone in 1823. Among those signing the Declaration of Independence were five Massachusetts citizens: John Adams, Samuel Adams, Elbridge Gerry, John Hancock, and Robert Treat Paine. They were among the innovators who created a whole new nation—the United States of America.

Samuel Adams (1722–1803) was a revolutionary with many bold ideas. "Among the natural rights of the colonists," he said, "are these: first, a right to life; secondly, to liberty; thirdly to property; together with the right to support and defend them in the best manner they can." Adams saw many of his innovative new ideas become part of the government of the new United States.

4. Better Living Through Science

1833, a view of Boston Harbor

As a coastal city Boston had always relied on the sea. The early 1800s brought a change to that. Growing troubles between Britain and the United States cut back trade between the two countries. When the British and the Americans went to war in 1812, trade fell off even more. Boston dockworkers and shipbuilders lost their jobs.

The war ended in 1815, and trade picked up again. Shipyards reopened. Workers returned to their jobs. The country, and Boston, enjoyed a time of prosperity in the 1820s and 1830s. Prosperity, often called "good times," meant that workers and merchants were making good money. Merchants began to spend some of their money on innovations.

Boston Manufacturing Company, founded in 1813, the first fully mechanized textile mill

One innovation that Boston merchants invested in was factories that made cloth and shoes by machine. Before this time, workers had made these goods by hand. Now innovative machines made them faster and cheaper.

Ice cutting at Spy Pond, West Cambridge

The merchant Frederic Tudor (1783–1864) found an innovative way to make money from the sea. He used his ships to transport winter ice from Massachusetts ponds to warm parts of the world. People laughed at him at first. How could Tudor be serious? Wouldn't the ice melt on the way? Well, it did at first. But Tudor improved the way he stored ice on his ships. Eventually he made a fortune carrying ice to places as far away as India.

While innovations moved forward in many ways, other areas made little progress. Medical surgery, for example, was stuck in place. Doctors mostly treated surface wounds. They couldn't work on more serious problems for one basic reason: when patients were thrashing about in pain, it was hard to operate on them.

The solution was to put the patient to sleep. But doctors had to be careful. If the sleep was too light, the patient awoke and started screaming in pain. If it was too deep, the patient died. As early as 1799, scientists in England had noted that if patients breathed in chemicals like nitrous oxide and ether, they got some relief from pain. But nobody thought of using these gases in surgery.

It was actually two dentists who led the way. In the early 1840s dentist Horace Wells had used nitrous oxide to relieve his patients' pain. He was invited to demonstrate his technique at Massachusetts General Hospital in 1845. In front of an audience

Early ether inhalers (inhale means to breathe in) were made from a globe of glass that was stuffed with sponges. Ether was poured onto the sponges. As the patient inhaled from the glass mouthpiece, he breathed air that was drawn over the ether-soaked sponges. This air, or ether fumes, put the patient to sleep.

of doctors, Wells had his patient breathe in the nitrous oxide. Once the patient seemed asleep, Wells went to work on him.

Unfortunately for Wells, his patient's sleep wasn't deep enough. Midway through the procedure, the man cried out in pain. Wells stopped operating at once, but it was too late. The doctors were already shaking their heads and muttering to one another. They were not impressed. The patient was clearly in pain. This approach was a fake, a humbug.

Wells was more than embarrassed. He was disgraced.

His mistake left room for William T. G. Morton to step up the next year. Morton was another dentist who had success putting patients to sleep. But he did not use nitrous oxide. He used ether. On October 16, 1846, in the same room Wells had used, Morton successfully anesthetized a patient. To anesthetize

Massachusetts General Hospital, left, and Harvard Medical School, right, 1853

John Collins Warren (1778–1856) helped start Massachusetts General Hospital, which opened in 1818. He was a pioneering surgeon, a doctor who operates on patients. He was always on the lookout for improvements in medical procedures. Warren was the doctor who invited both Horace Wells and William T. G. Morton to demonstrate their techniques.

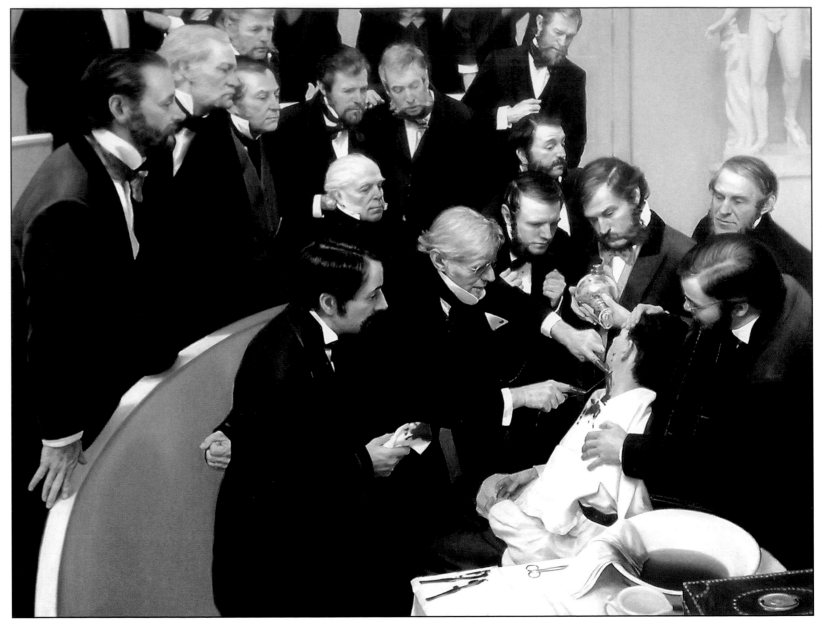

A mural at Massachusetts General Hospital showing an early operation using ether

means to put the patient into a painless sleep. Surgeon John Collins Warren removed a tumor as a crowd of curious doctors looked on.

When the patient awakened, he was asked how much pain he had felt. None, the patient replied. "Gentlemen, this is no humbug!" Warren declared. The ability to relieve pain changed the way surgery was performed. A new and innovative medical field called anesthesiology was born.

Horace Wells (1815–1848) does not get the credit he deserves for pioneering the use of anesthesia in operations. Sadly, he gave up medicine after the failure of his demonstration and died a very unhappy death only a few years later.

John Collins Warren turned an innovative idea into a practical way to treat patients

Boston led the way in more than just medicine. Boston innovators pioneered new ideas in education, in the fight against slavery, and in useful inventions for home and factory.

Horace Mann (1796–1859) was a member of the Massachusetts Board of Education. He was responsible for a number of positive changes, including separating students into different grades by age and establishing a six-month minimum school year.

Classroom in Boston Latin School

Perkins School Children

America's first school for the blind opened in Boston in 1832. Its director was Samuel Gridley Howe. The next year the school moved to a larger building, a home owned by merchant Thomas Perkins. Perkins later agreed to sell the home and donate the money to the school if the city raised $50,000 for the school's support. The money was collected in just six weeks. The school, now called the Perkins School, still operates today on a large campus in the Boston suburb of Watertown.

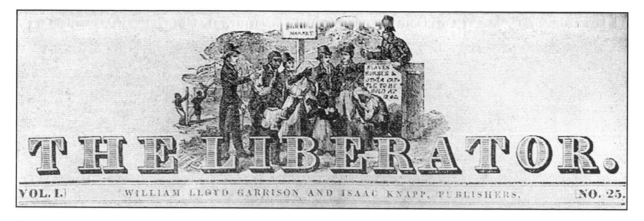

VOL. I. WILLIAM LLOYD GARRISON AND ISAAC KNAPP, PUBLISHERS. NO. 25.

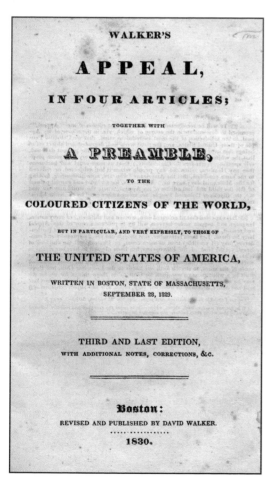

WALKER'S

APPEAL,

IN FOUR ARTICLES;

TOGETHER WITH

A PREAMBLE,

TO THE

COLOURED CITIZENS OF THE WORLD,

BUT IN PARTICULAR, AND VERY EXPRESSLY, TO THOSE OF

THE UNITED STATES OF AMERICA,

WRITTEN IN BOSTON, STATE OF MASSACHUSETTS,
SEPTEMBER 28, 1829.

THIRD AND LAST EDITION,
WITH ADDITIONAL NOTES, CORRECTIONS, &c.

Boston:
REVISED AND PUBLISHED BY DAVID WALKER.
1830.

The antislavery, or abolitionist, movement started in Boston. To abolish means to get rid of something. Abolitionists both black and white wanted to do away with slavery. Some people felt that Boston abolitionists were instrumental in causing the American Civil War.

Elias Howe (1819–1867) invented the first sewing machine in 1846 while working in a factory in Cambridge. Unfortunately his design was too expensive for the average home. Isaac Singer got most of the glory for successfully marketing sewing machines to the public. But Singer paid Howe a royalty, a part of the profit, on every machine he sold.

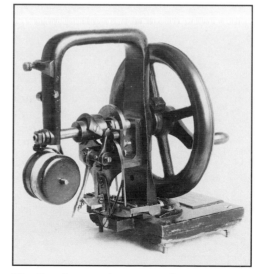

Elias Howe's original sewing machine

5. Hearing the Call of the Future

View of Back Bay from the Massachusetts State House, 1858

Boston's population jumped from 177,840 in 1860 to 362,839 in 1880 as other towns asked to become part of the city.

As the United States grew bigger and bigger, Boston got farther and farther away from the center of things. The 1840s and 1850s were a time of rapid growth for America's cities. Boston, like other cities, grew for several reasons. First, people were moving from farms to cities, where innovation had created jobs in the new mills and factories. Second, port cities grew because immigrants settled there. Immigrants are people who move from one country to another. Most of Boston's immigrants came from Ireland. Boston also grew because nearby towns wanted to become part of the city. And Boston used innovation to create more land for the city.

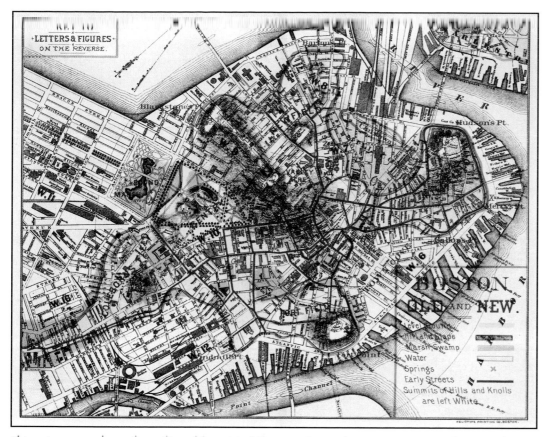

This unique map shows the outline of the original Shawmut Peninsula over an 1880 map of Boston. The yellow areas are level ground, brown indicates hilly areas, and green shows marshland and swamps

In 1860 Elizabeth Peabody (1804–1894) established the first American public kindergarten in Boston. This was another example of a Boston innovation in education.

Using new technology like steam shovels and railroads, Boston filled in swampland in an area called Back Bay. At times, as many as twenty-five trainloads of gravel were dumped each day into the bay. When the project was done, Boston was thirty times bigger than it had been in 1630. This was due to filling in the land and to new towns that became part of the city.

Some of Boston's growing population may have tried a new dessert at the Parker House Hotel, which opened in 1855. The Boston cream pie was actually a cake with chocolate frosting and a custard filling. But the name stuck. The hotel was also the first in Boston to have hot and cold running water.

A Boston innovation in book publishing was *Little Women* by Louisa May Alcott (1832–1888). Before this book was published in 1869, most children's books taught lessons in how to behave. *Little Women* was an interesting story that children could actually enjoy.

Scientific advancements were encouraged when Massachusetts Institute of Technology admitted its first students in 1865. Here students learned by solving real-world problems instead of just reading books.

Innovative technology was changing the way Americans lived. The telegraph, for example, let people communicate across the country almost instantly. Most people were amazed and happy that they could send messages in Morse code over the wires.

But not Alexander Graham Bell. He wondered if voice messages could also be sent over wires. His natural curiosity was not easily satisfied. Born in Scotland in 1847, Bell came from a family

THIS MODEL OF BELL'S FIRST TELEPHONE IS A DUPLICATE OF THE INSTRUMENT THROUGH WHICH SPEECH SOUNDS WERE FIRST TRANSMITTED ELECTRICALLY, 1875.

Alexander Graham Bell

SCHOOL OF VOCAL PHYSIOLOGY,
18 Beacon Street, Boston, Mass.,
CONDUCTED BY
A. GRAHAM BELL,

A notice for a school Bell started in 1872 in Boston to help people with speech problems

very interested in the power of voice. His father studied speech defects. His mother was deaf, yet she still became a talented pianist. Young Aleck found he could talk to his mother by speaking in low tones very near her face. Although she could not hear him, she could understand some of his words through the vibrations passing through her head.

The inventor's wife, Mabel Hubbard Bell, holding a tensiometer, an instrument that measures tension, attached to cable from a flying kite

Alexander Graham Bell and others with a tetrahedral, or four-sided, kite "Cygnet I." Bell designed, made, and tested kites of different shapes that he thought could be used for man-assisted flight

Alexander Graham Bell (1847–1922) was curious about many areas of science. The fortune that he made from the telephone allowed him to investigate a number of them. In his later years he explored such different areas as airplanes and sheep breeding. He also helped found *National Geographic* magazine.

Bell came to Boston in 1871. His job was to teach at the Boston School for Deaf Mutes. Because of his mother's deafness, he was very curious about the way sound traveled to the human ear. Bell was also an inventor. At first he experimented on improvements for the telegraph. He worked in a lab where another young inventor, Thomas Edison, had done investigations of his own just a few years before.

Birthplace of the telephone, 109 Court Street, Boston. On the top floor of this building in 1875, Professor Bell carried on his experiments and first succeeded in transmitting speech by electricity

Lewis Latimer (1848–1928), the son of runaway slaves, grew up near Boston in Chelsea. As an inventor he contributed to developing both Bell's telephone and Edison's lightbulb. With Bell, he helped prepare the drawings for the telephone patent application.
(A patent gives an inventor the right to be the only person selling his invention.) A few years later Latimer improved Edison's lightbulb by introducing a carbon filament, or threadlike conductor, to carry the electrical current. This extended the life of Edison's lightbulb from minutes to hours, which led directly to the practical adoption of electric lights.

Poster advertising Columbia bicycles

In 1877 Colonel Albert Pope (1843–1909) founded the Pope Manufacturing Company at 45 High Street in Boston to make bicycles. Pope had seen a two-wheeled machine at Philadelphia's Centennial Exhibition the year before. By the 1890s, people everywhere were riding new models of Pope's invention.

Bell made some progress, creating a kind of telegraph that could send more than one message at a time over a single wire. It was an encouraging development. A wire could send many message sounds at the same time. Bell wondered if a wire could also transmit all the complicated sounds that made up the human voice.

In 1875 Bell and his assistant Thomas Watson began trying to transmit the human voice over wires. Months passed as they tried different ideas. On March 10, 1876, in the middle of an experiment in his Boston laboratory, Bell spilled some acid on his clothes. "Mr. Watson, come here! I want you!" he called out.

Replicas of the magnetic transmitter and receiver exhibited at the Philadelphia Centennial Exposition of 1876

Robert Paget (1836–1878) introduced the swan boats to the Boston Public Garden in 1877. The boats are powered by a paddle wheel driven by a bicycle-like mechanism. The original boats carried 8 passengers. Current ones can hold up to 20. Paget's family still runs the business after more than 100 years.

These words carried over the wire to where Watson was working in another room. And Watson heard them! Bell's invention, the telephone, finally worked.

Later that year Bell introduced the telephone at the Centennial Exhibition in Philadelphia. The new invention was the talk of the town. Within a few years that talk was traveling on wires from coast to coast.

Thomas Edison (1847–1931) is known as the Wizard of Menlo Park, which is in New Jersey. However, he started his career in Boston. There he created his first invention, an automatic vote counter, in 1869.

6. Home Improvements

First subway being built

As Boston kept growing, the challenges facing the city kept growing, too. More people meant more roads and sewers and schools and traffic. The city streets were jammed with people, horses, carts, wagons, and a recent innovation—the trolley. Boston soon came up with another innovation—the subway. Now trolleys could travel along tracks below the city's streets and move people quickly from place to place.

It went without saying, however, that innovators were men. Women did not have a head for such things. At least that's what most people believed!

Young Ellen Swallow held a different view. Growing up in rural Dunstable, Massachusetts, she was educated at home until her family moved to neighboring Westford. She was eager to learn but was unable to attend college until 1868, when she was twenty-five. By that time she had saved enough money to enroll at three-year-old Vassar College, in Poughkeepsie, New York, one of the first colleges for women.

The first trolley in the Tremont Street tunnel, September 1, 1897

Swallow liked science courses, especially chemistry. And she was good at them. She also thought she knew what she wanted from the world. As she wrote to her parents, she had no desire to "be one of the delicate little dolls or the silly fools who make up the bulk of American women, slaves to society and fashion."

But after graduating in 1870, Swallow was unable to find a job suitable for her scientific skills. So she decided

The first subway in America was completed in Boston in 1898 after three years of construction. Did anyone care? Well, the new streetcar subway carried more than 100,000 riders on its first day. London had a subway already, but this was the first one in America. It was built 7 years before construction was begun on a subway in New York City.

Ellen Swallow Richards (1842–1911) was a pioneer in the field of home economics. As one of the first female professional chemists, she was also the country's first widely recognized woman scientist.

Women's Laboratory at MIT

to continue her education at Massachusetts Institute of Technology (MIT). MIT had been founded in 1861 and began admitting students in 1865. It had never enrolled a woman. Swallow was accepted as a special student and did not have to pay tuition. She later learned that this was not an act of kindness. Instead, she wrote, it allowed the president to "say I was not a student, should any of the trustees or students make a fuss about my presence."

As director of the Boston Cooking School from 1892 to 1902, Fannie Farmer influenced how Americans cooked. The Fannie Farmer Cookbook *is still being published*

After graduating in 1873, Swallow continued her studies. She also married Professor Robert Richards and worked to help establish a laboratory at MIT for teaching chemistry courses to women. She analyzed water and sewage systems for the Commonwealth of Massachusetts and pioneered environmental safety before there was a name for it.

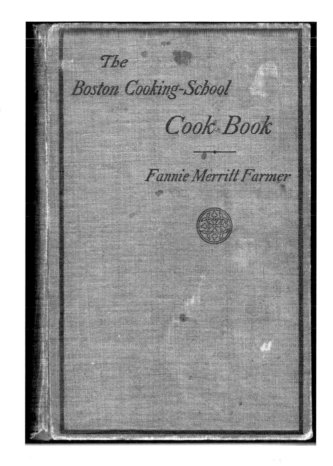

Fannie Merritt Farmer (1857–1915) was another Boston innovator. She took a very scientific approach to the subject of cooking. In 1896 she published *The Boston Cooking-School Cook Book*, the first cookbook to list precise amounts for every ingredient in a recipe. Farmer also taught the value of proper nutrition. "I certainly feel that the time is not far distant," she said, "when a knowledge of the principles of diet will be an essential part of one's education."

Boston's Symphony Hall opened in 1900. It was the home of the Boston Symphony Orchestra and another example of a Boston innovation. The new science of acoustics—how sound travels—helped the builders design the flooring, the walls, and even the seat covers to provide the best sound possible. More than a hundred years later, Symphony Hall remains one of the world's finest places to hear music.

Ellen Swallow Richards also brought science into the home through the new field of home economics. The idea was to apply the same scientific standards used in biology or chemistry to such domestic pursuits as cleaning, nutrition, and physical fitness. Just because a woman did housework or cooked didn't mean she shouldn't be thinking and learning. Women, Richards protested, were discouraged from using their brains even at home. "You cannot make women contented with cooking and cleaning," she said, "and you need not try."

Looking ahead to the future, Richards saw modern women using their heads as well as their hands. All they had to do was follow her example.

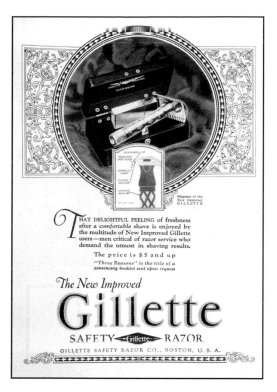

Before King C. Gillette (1855–1932) came along, shaving meant using a straight-edged razor. It was like shaving with the edge of a knife. Gillette invented a safety razor with a disposable blade in 1901. The Gillette Company, now part of Procter and Gamble, still manufactures razors in South Boston, less than a mile from its first shop.

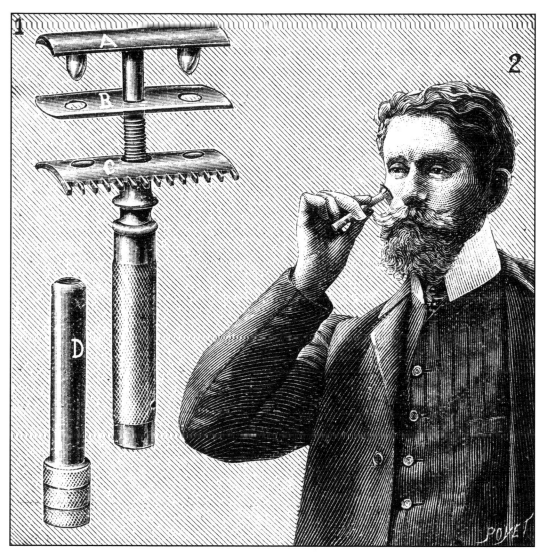

7. Power Plays

Huntington Avenue Grounds during first World Series, 1903

Huntington Avenue Grounds, 1903

Ruth Wakefield (1905–1977) owned the Toll House Inn in a Boston suburb. One day in the early 1930s she experimented with a cookie recipe by dropping pieces of semisweet chocolate into the dough. She expected the chocolate to melt right in during baking. Instead it softened but held its shape. The result? The first chocolate-chip cookie, another Boston innovation.

The Great Depression of the 1930s hit Boston as hard as everywhere else. As stocks fell, many banks lost the value of their investments. Without those investments the banks could no longer give customers the money in their accounts. Years of savings were lost. At the same time hundreds of companies and factories closed.

James Michael Curley, who served one of his four terms as Boston's mayor from 1930 to 1934, tried to keep jobs going. But with businesses failing and tax dollars shrinking, he could do only

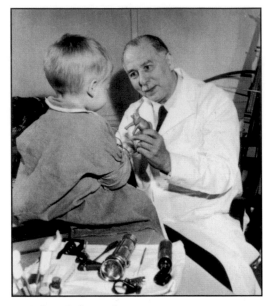

Dr. Sidney Farber with a patient

Dr. Sidney Farber (1903–1973) was an innovative Boston doctor who treated cancer in children. He was the first doctor to test on children a drug that cured them of leukemia. He helped create the Jimmy Fund in 1948. "Jimmy," a name given to a real 12-year-old cancer patient of Dr. Farber's, made an appeal on the radio that brought in money for fund-raising for cancer research.

so much. Workers lost their jobs. Families lost their homes. Many people did not have enough to eat.

During these hard times a few things helped brighten people's lives. The movies were one form of escape. Another was sports, especially baseball. The Boston Red Sox had won six World Series in the first twenty years of the century. But the team had not done so well since trading away Babe Ruth after the 1918 season.

In 1939 a rookie left fielder joined the team. Ted Williams had grown up in San Diego, and baseball had always been the center of his life. Even in high school he stood out, playing on teams with much older players.

Some people said that playing baseball well was just a matter of good luck. If you were born with talent, you were all set. Players practiced, of course, but they didn't think about their skills in a scientific way. (This was the era, after all, when Babe Ruth supposedly ate twelve hot dogs between the games of a doubleheader.)

Ted Williams looked at his talent differently. "There has always been a saying in baseball that you can't make a hitter," he said, "but I think you can improve a hitter."

Aerial view of Children's Hospital and Harvard Medical School in Boston in 1921

The Jimmy Fund was Ted Williams's favorite charity. It helped support what is now the Dana-Farber Cancer Institute at Children's Hospital Boston. The Jimmy Fund was an early pioneer in enlisting celebrities, especially sports figures, to help with fundraising. It remains an active and effective charity today.

Ted Williams (1918–2002) also served as a fighter pilot in both World War II and the Korean War.

And he set out to prove it. Williams didn't just swing away and hope for the best. He was also known for his sharp eyesight and patience at the plate. Williams divided the strike zone into small areas. He knew which areas were the ones where he could hit the ball most effectively. Williams rarely struck out. "Hitting is 50 percent above the shoulders," he said, meaning that he hit with his brain as well as his bat. His innovative ideas about his sport made him one of America's finest baseball players.

Ted Williams hits one out, about 1948

Williams was also a special hitter because he hit for both power and accuracy. He hit 521 home runs and had a lifetime .344 batting average.

Carl Yastrzemski, the man who followed Williams as a left fielder for the Red Sox in 1961, had this to say about him: "They can talk about Babe Ruth and Ty Cobb and Rogers Hornsby and Lou Gehrig and Joe DiMaggio and Stan Musial and all the rest, but I'm sure not one of them could hold cards and spades to Williams in his sheer knowledge of hitting. He studied hitting the way a broker studies the stock market and could spot at a glance mistakes that others couldn't see in a week."

Ted Williams wanted to be remembered as "the greatest hitter who ever lived." So far, as the last man to hit over .400 in a season (.406 in 1941), he can still lay claim to that title.

During World War II scientists at Boston's Raytheon Company began to build electrical tubes used in radar systems. One of the scientists, Percy Spencer (1894–1970), saw that the heat from the tubes caused a nearby chocolate bar to melt. This discovery led to the development of the microwave oven. The first ones were as big as refrigerators and cost $100,000. But by the late 1960s, they were small enough and cheap enough to start showing up in everyday kitchens.

Bostonian Edwin Land (1909–1991) was the innovator behind the instant photograph. He started the Polaroid Corporation, which introduced the Polaroid Land Camera in 1948. Until digital cameras came along in the 1990s, Polaroid cameras were the popular choice for those who wanted to see their pictures right away.

8. Number Crunching

The Stata Center at Massachusetts Institute of Technology under construction

In the last half of the twentieth century, Boston finally grew up—and up and up. Before that time the city's skyscrapers were few and far between. The Custom House, built in 1915, was sixteen stories, less than half the height of New York's Empire State Building (which opened nineteen years later). And the old John Hancock Tower, built in 1947, was actually a foot shorter than the Custom House.

But starting with the Prudential Tower in 1964 (fifty-two stories), the city started making up for lost time. The new John Hancock Tower in 1976 (sixty stories) and other new buildings in the financial district dramatically raised the skyline.

The Leonard P. Zakim Bunker Hill Bridge

In 1950 Elma Lewis (1921–2004) founded the Elma Lewis School of Fine Arts. She was an innovative educator who taught fine arts to neighborhood children. Over the years the school has given thousands of inner-city children the chance to learn art, dance, and drama.

Boston's biggest construction project was the Big Dig. This huge road project began in the 1980s and took more than twenty years to complete. Its new bridges and tunnels included the Leonard P. Zakim Bunker Hill Bridge over the Charles River and the Ted Williams Tunnel under Boston Harbor. But the key part of the project was putting more than a mile of interstate highway underground. Before, this highway had cut the downtown area in two. The waterfront was now reunited with the rest of downtown.

Computer board

During the last half of the twentieth century Boston emerged as a center for high-tech industries. These new companies built and used computers in many new ways. Massachusetts was the birthplace of many computer innovations. In fact the first modern computer was developed at MIT in 1928.

These early computers were as big as houses. Year after year, computers became both smaller and more powerful. By the 1970s the smallest computers fit on a desk. This was great for users. But nobody had figured out how to make these machines appeal to a wide audience.

To be popular, a computer had to have a system for letting people do a difficult job easily. Programs that can do that are called software, or applications. And a "killer app" is a really neat application that everyone wants.

In 1969 the Department of Defense was looking for someone to develop a way to send and receive data between different computers. A team from a small firm named Bolt, Beranek and Newman developed a system called ARPANET. This successful system, another Boston innovation, led to the creation of the Internet.

The attic where VisiCalc was created

Ray Tomlinson (1941–) was a scientist at Bolt, Beranek and Newman in the early 1970s. He was working on computer programs that would allow the transmission of electronic mail. He chose the @ sign to separate the user's name from the computer address. Why? "Mostly it seemed like a neat idea," he later explained.

Dan Bricklin wasn't thinking about killer apps when he started programming in high school in the late 1960s. He was just interested in computers. And like any engineering student (he graduated from MIT in 1973), Bricklin used a calculator. But calculators were limited. They could only do individual calculations. They couldn't show how different numbers related to one another in a chart or table. A calculator screen was way too small for that.

In 1974 Kip Tiernan (1925–), another Boston innovator, founded Rosie's Place, the first drop-in and emergency shelter for poor and homeless women in the United States. Again Boston led the way with a new idea for helping people in communities everywhere.

But a personal computer's screen wasn't too small at all.

Bricklin was a student at Harvard Business School in 1978. He started using a recent innovation called a mouse to move numbers around on a screen. When he changed a number in one box of a row or column, the program would automatically recalculate, or refigure, all the numbers affected by that change. He called his innovation a "spreadsheet."

That summer he started a company, Software Arts, with his friend Bob Frankston. A year later they announced their new spreadsheet product, VisiCalc, to the public. The VisiCalc slogan was "How did you ever do without it?" As things turned out, very few businesses could. Within a few months the personal-computer revolution was on its way.

In 1964, MIT professor Dr. Amar G. Bose (1929–) started the Bose Corporation to bring innovative sound systems to the public. His first important product was the Bose 901 loudspeaker system. It reproduces music in the home so that it sounds more like the live music heard in a concert hall.

Julia Child (1912–2004) learned about French cooking in the years after World War II. She enjoyed cooking and teaching people how to cook. Her great innovative idea was a cooking show on Boston's public television station. Her show was so popular that she changed the way Americans cooked and ate.

Copley Square, Boston

As you can see, Boston has been a busy place for almost four hundred years. The people here have come up with big ideas, small ideas, and who-would-have-thought-of-that ideas. And Boston isn't done yet. New notions and breakthroughs will continue to pop up. Some will happen through careful planning and experiments. Others will be totally unexpected. That's what makes the whole process of discovery so exciting. In the twenty-first century, Boston will likely inspire new thinkers to produce innovations we can't even imagine yet. Who knows what will happen next?

Suggested Reading

Borden, Louise. *Sleds on Boston Common: A Story from the American Revolution.* Illustrated by Robert Andrew Parker. New York: Margaret K. McElderry, 2000.

Carlson, Laurie. *Queen of Inventions: How the Sewing Machine Changed the World.* Brookfield, CT: Milbrook Press, 2003.

Forbes, Esther. *Johnny Tremain.* Boston: Houghton Mifflin Co., 1944.

Fritz, Jean. *Will You Sign Here, John Hancock?* Illustrated by Trina Schart Hyman. New York: Coward, McCann & Geohegan, 1976.

Harlow, Joan Hiatt. *Joshua's Song.* New York: Margaret K. McElderry, 2001.

Hopkinson, Deborah. *Fannie in the Kitchen: The Whole Story from Soup to Nuts of How Fannie Farmer Invented Recipes with Precise Measurements.* Illustrated by Nancy Carpenter. New York: Aladdin Publishing, 2004.

Lasky, Kathryn. *Home at Last: Sofia's Immigrant Diary* (My America Series). New York: Scholastic, 2003.

MacLeod, Elizabeth. *Alexander Graham Bell: An Inventive Life.* Toronto: Kids Can Press, 1999.

McKendry, Joe. *Beneath the Streets of Boston: Building America's First Subway.* Boston: David R. Godine, Publisher, 2005.

Rubin, Susan Goldman. *Toilets, Toasters, and Telephones: The How and Why of Everyday Objects.* San Diego: Harcourt, 1998.

Wood, James Playsted. *Boston.* Illustrated by Robert Frankenberg. New York: The Seabury Press, 1967.

It Happened in Boston

1624 William Blackstone landed at Plymouth and later became the first European settler of Boston

1630 On September 17, the town of Boston founded by John Winthrop and his followers

1634 Beacon erected on "Beacon" Hill

1639 Stephen Daye set up the first printing press of the British American colonies in Cambridge
America's first post office opened at Fairbanks Tavern

1640 Stephen Daye published the first English-language book in the colonies, *Bay Psalm Book*

1679 First building code established to prevent fires

1728 First paper mill in America opened in Dorchester Lower Mills

1760 Sons of Liberty founded at Green Dragon Tavern

1765 America's first chocolate mill (Baker Chocolate) built in Dorchester

1803 The new Merrimack Canal built, linking northern Massachusetts and southern New Hampshire to Boston

1815 Handel and Haydn Society (oldest music society in America) founded

1826 Union Oyster House opened (oldest restaurant in America still operating in same location)

1827 America's first horticultural society (Massachusetts Horticultural Society) formed

1832 The New England Anti-Slavery Society in Boston formed to help slaves escape to Canada

1837 First elevator in America installed in Scollay Square hotel

1841 Transcendentalists created Brook Farm in West Roxbury

1851 First YMCA in America founded in Boston

1855 The Parker House opened (oldest hotel continuously operating in America)

1870 Museum of Fine Arts founded

1879 Christian Science Church founded by Mary Baker Eddy

1882 Hotel Vendome was the first commercial building in America illuminated with electric lights

1884 Frederick Law Olmsted started "Emerald Necklace," the country's first park system

1890 Back Bay completely filled in

1892 Pledge of Allegiance written by Francis Bellamy at 142 Berkeley Street

1903 America's first football stadium, Harvard Stadium, opened

1954 Boston's Freedom Trail becomes first self-guided walking tour in America

1976 The first First Night celebrated

1991 Big Dig construction project begun to reunify Boston's neighborhoods

2000 Led by Eric Lander, a scientist at Whitehead Institute in Cambridge, the Human Genome Project completes mapping of the full set of genes in the human body

Index

Photo Credits